T0023232

Getting bird sounds is as easy as:

1.

Download the
FREE
Uncover Everything
app

2.

Open the app
and tap **"SCAN"**

3.

Point your phone at
the image and hold it
still for three seconds
until the **red** bounding
box turns **green** to
hear the bird's call.

chirp *chirp*

chirp

Hear the birds' calls right from your mobile device! Here's how:
(You will only need to download Uncover Everything once.)

---

1. Using your smartphone, **download** and install the free **Uncover Everything app** from either the Google Play or Apple App Store.
2. Open the app, and tap on the **scan icon** in the middle of the screen.
3. Carefully point your phone's camera at the image of the bird, and hold it still for three seconds until the red bounding box turns green.
4. **Watch and listen** as your book comes to life with calls from each bird!

TIPS: Make sure your phone has a strong connection to the internet and the volume is turned all the way up! Still having trouble? Hold your phone very still, and make sure the area is well lit.

For help or additional tips, contact us at kermitcummingsbooks@gmail.com.

Apple devices must have iOS 7.0 or higher.   **Android devices must be version 4.0 or higher.**

Special thanks to David Cummings, Lang Elliott / LangElliott.com, and Render Logic Studios.

A BACKYARD BIRDING
ADVENTURE

What's in Your Yard?

Kermit Cummings

Illustrations by
Holly Weinstein

BROWN BOOKS KIDS

A Backyard Birding Adventure
What's in Your Yard?

Brown Books Kids
Dallas, TX / New York, NY
www.BrownBooksKids.com
(972) 381-0009

A New Era in Publishing®

Publisher's Cataloging-In-Publication Data

Names: Cummings, Kermit, author. | Weinstein, Holly, illustrator.
Title: A backyard birding adventure : what's in your yard? / Kermit Cummings ; illustrations by Holly Weinstein.
Other Titles: What's in your yard?
Description: Dallas, TX : Brown Books Kids, [2015] | Interest age level: 004-008. | A smartphone app featuring typical bird calls is available for download. | Summary: Introduces your child to the world of birds, focusing on easy-to-see bird species.
Identifiers: ISBN 9781612542362
Subjects: LCSH: Birds--Identification--Juvenile literature. | Bird watching--Juvenile literature. | CYAC: Birds--Identification. | Bird watching.
Classification: LCC QL676.2 .C86 2015 | DDC 598--dc23

ISBN 978-1-61254-236-2
LCCN 2014960361

Printed in the United States
10 9 8 7 6 5 4 3 2

For more information or to contact the author, please go to www.KermitCummings.com.

Photo Credits

Carolina Chickadee...© James Giroux/JamesAGiroux.com
American Robin ....© Arthur Morris/VIREO
Blue Jay ....© Glen Bartley/VIREO
Carolina Wren ....© James Giroux/JamesAGiroux.com
Downy Woodpecker ....© James Giroux/JamesAGiroux.com
Eastern Bluebird...© Garth McElroy/VIREO
Northern Cardinal ....© James Giroux/JamesAGiroux.com
Northern Mockingbird ....© Doug Wechsler/VIREO
Tufted Titmouse..© James Giroux/JamesAGiroux.com
Mourning Dove...© Laure Neish/VIREO

In memory of my mother, Elsie Crawford Cummings, who read to her children when they were young and instilled in them a love of words, rhymes, and the wonders of nature.

Acknowledgments

I am grateful to many people for their help in bringing this book to fruition. First in line is my wife Dorothy, without whose unwavering persistence and encouragement this book would never have been written. Dorothy's son, James Giroux, has not only been a co-conspirator but the provider of five of the stunning photographs featured in the book. James's wife Debbie, daughter Julia, and son Aaron all pitched in with helpful suggestions, as did my daughter Cathy Cummings Powell, Dorothy's daughter Jennifer, and her son, Aiden. Aiden suggested the book's title.

Finally, from my very first contact with Brown Books, Sherry LeVine, Kathy Penny, and the rest of the superlative Brown Books team have been enthusiastic helpers and supporters in this effort. To all of the above, I send my heartfelt thanks!

Let's learn about birds;
it's not all that hard.
Let's start with a few
we can find in our yard!

We'll look, and we'll listen;
oh how to begin?
Let's make a list
and find our first ten!

There's a bird on the ground
with a rusty-red breast.
She's looking for worms—
at least that's my guess.

An **AMERICAN ROBIN**,
she nests in a tree.
Hunting worms on the lawn,
she's easy to see!

Daddy Robin sings in
the spring of the year.
His bright, cheerful whistles
are delightful to hear!

AMERICAN ROBIN

It's easy to tell when
BLUE JAY's around.
He's big and he's loud—
hear his brash sound?

"Jaaay! Jaaay! Jaaay!"
as if to say,
"All you other birds,
out of my way!"

Dressed all in blue,
he's handsome, as well,
but "he" might be the mommy;
you never can tell!

BLUE JAY

Listen! Hear that sound?
"Chick-a-dee-dee-dee."
Look, there they are!
A pair in the tree.

Black cap and bib,
accenting the gray,
the **CAROLINA CHICKADEE**
is a treat any day!

These tiny acrobats,
always on the go,
deserve applause from us
for putting on a show!

CAROLINA CHICKADEE

13

Hear the **CAROLINA WREN**?
A friendly little bird,
they like our yards and porches
and are often seen and heard.

Rusty birds with cocked-up tails,
they're nosy as can be.
They hop about, sing their songs,
and keep us company.

They like to nest
in a sheltered site.
A carport shelf
would be just right!

CAROLINA WREN

Do you hear pecking?
Look, there on the limb.
It's little **DOWNY WOODPECKER**,
so neat and oh so trim!

Woodpeckers dig their homes
in trees both short and tall.
They peck and peck, "Rat-tat-tat,"
and whinny when they call.

These birds roam the woods,
eating bugs that hurt our trees.
They're real heroes; don't you think?
We could use more friends like these!

16

DOWNY WOODPECKER

17

Look! There are two birds on the line,
shoulders hunched and looking down.
A soft "Cher-ree," they call
as they flutter to the ground.

Blue, blue back and reddish breast,
BLUEBIRDS nest in cavities.
At times they're found in birdhouses
or even holes in big, old trees.

They guard their nests
and patrol the yard.
When competitors come,
they'll chase them hard!

EASTERN BLUEBIRD

Ah, there goes a **CARDINAL**,
a bird of crimson hue!
This striking male and his soft-toned mate
are a thrill for us to view.

Cardinals eat from our feeders.
They crack seeds with cone-shaped bills.
Their songs ring loud and clear in spring
as they greet us with their trills.

This handsome bird builds his nest
in a bush or shrub or tree.
The young ones hatch and beg for food,
quite a sight for us to see!

NORTHERN CARDINAL

Hear Mr. **MOCKINGBIRD**
with his ever-changing song?
He's a copycat and sings the tunes
of a mighty feathered throng!

Mockingbirds are flashy fliers,
all decked out in gray and white.
They sing the long, long days away
and sometimes sing at night!

Mockingbirds protect their young;
let's not go too near.
They chase big birds and cats and squirrels,
and *nothing* do they fear!

NORTHERN MOCKINGBIRD

23

Here's a little **TITMOUSE**,
a favorite bird indeed!
He pecks between his toes
to crack his sunflower seed.

"Hurry, hurry, hurry,"
he calls incessantly.
His mate is out to build her nest
in a cozy cavity.

Dressed in gray,
she's pretty classy
with a perky crest
that's downright sassy!

TUFTED TITMOUSE

MOURNING DOVE

What's that plump bird there?
See it in the tree?
Grayish brown with a pointed tail,
I wonder what it could be?

Oh! It's a **MOURNING DOVE**!
Hear that soft, sad sound?
These birds nest in trees
but are often on the ground.

They poke about on short pink legs
and look so calm and slow.
But make a sound and *whoosh*,
they're off, as on they swiftly go!

I've enjoyed our walk,
but now it must end.
We've learned about birds;
what fun it has been!

Next time, we'll look, and we'll listen;
we'll search high and low
and list some new birds
wherever we may go!

A Note to Parents on
Getting Started as a Birdwatcher

Birdwatching, or "birding," is a pastime pursued by millions of people around the world, and it is a great way to bring families together. Birding gives parents the chance to engage their children in activities that are educational and entertaining.

If you are interested in getting to know more about the world of birds, start where you live. Learn about the birds in your neighborhood. Once you start paying attention, you might be surprised at how many are out there!

The first step is to put up a bird feeder. A mixture of 90% sunflower seeds and 10% small grains will make your backyard a popular spot for feathered visitors. Another must is a birdbath. Birds use birdbaths as an important resource at which to bathe and drink.

"How do I know what I'm seeing?" is a question that comes to mind, especially if you are a beginner. The technological explosion of the last dozen years has ushered in "apps" and devices that can literally put every bird you are ever going to see at your fingertips, complete with the sounds it makes. However, my advice would be to buy a field guide for the birds in your part of the country. Spend some time learning about the differences that separate the various groups or "families" of birds. These guides also have excellent articles dealing with the anatomy or "topography" of birds.

A piece of equipment that all birders need is a good quality binocular. The binocular opens up a whole new world of beauty. Most of the time, little birds that flit around in the upper branches of trees can't be seen without one.

Once you become acquainted with your binocular and your book, you can begin to keep up with what is happening in your backyard. You are now ready for untold hours of pleasure.

Another facet of birding to consider is listing and record-keeping. Not all birders keep records of the bird species they see, but many do. A "life list," a list of all the species you see from the day you start recording, is very common. This list, which can be kept in a simple notebook, may include a life list number (beginning with the number "1," designating the first bird seen), the common name of the bird, the date and location where seen, plus any other details you might want to add. In addition, some people keep yard lists, annual lists, county lists, state lists, and so on.

The choice of how much or how little you want to get involved in birding is yours to make. There is a world of fun waiting just outside your doorstep!

About the Author

Kermit C. Cummings grew up in North Texas and graduated from Southern Methodist University in 1955 with a degree in business administration. Upon graduation, he was employed by Procter & Gamble Manufacturing Co. and spent his entire career with that firm, working in Dallas, TX, Sacramento, CA, Augusta, GA, and Alexandria, LA, before retiring in 1993.

While living in Augusta, and convalescing following a surgery, a friend loaned him a copy of *Song and Garden Birds of North America.* Although Cummings considered himself aware of the natural world and the outdoors, he was amazed at the number of bird species to which he was oblivious.

The same friend also introduced him to the concept of "life listing," which is a personal listing of bird species, numbered in the order seen following the creation of the list. Other details usually include date and location of the sighting. Keeping a list appealed to his competitive nature, and it didn't take long for Cummings to become a self-taught birder.

Through the ensuing years and into retirement, Cummings has pursued his hobby far and wide, looking for birds wherever his travels have taken him. He has influenced many among his family and friends to join the huge number of people in this country interested in and dedicated to the pursuit of new birds for their life lists.

Cummings has been an active member of a number of birding-related organizations, including the Louisiana Ornithological Society, where he served as a member of the board of directors for several years. He now resides in Huntsville, TX, with his wife Dorothy.

About the Illustrator

Holly Weinstein received her BFA degree from the College of Art and Design at Lesley University, and she has since illustrated several picture books. She lives in Dallas, TX, with her husband and two children. She is proud to say that she can now identify all of the blue jays, mockingbirds, cardinals, and woodpeckers in her own backyard.